Celebrating
Midday
Prayer

MOWBRAY

Mowbray
A Cassell imprint
Villiers House, 41-47 Strand, London WC2N 5JE, UK
387 Park Avenue South, New York, NY 10016-8810, USA

This booklet is an extract from *Celebrating Common Prayer*,
© The European Province of the Society of Saint Francis 1992
and published by Mowbray (with some minor adjustments).

Text and typography:
© The European Province of the Society of Saint Francis 1994

Editor: Brother Tristam SSF

ISBN 0-264-67347-6
    0-264-67349-2 (pack of 10)

Gratitude is expressed to the following for permission to reproduce
material, some of which is copyright:

Charles Mortimer Guilbert, Custodian of the *Book of Common Prayer* of
the Episcopal Church in the USA, 1979, for use of *The Psalms*, on which
no copyright is claimed;

© The Division of Christian Education of the National Council of the
Churches of Christ in the USA: scriptural texts from the *Revised
Standard Version*, 1946, 1952 & 1971, and the *New Revised Standard
Version*, 1989, of the Bible;

© The Central Board of Finance of the Church of England: prayers from
The Alternative Service Book 1980 with the attribution 2; and a prayer
from *The Promise of His Glory*, Church House Publishing & Mowbray, 1991,
with the attribution 3;

© David Silk, Bishop of Ballarat: prayers from *Prayers for Use at the
Alternative Services*, Mowbray, 1980 and 1986, with the attribution 4;

Prayers with the attribution 1 were newly written by SSF.

Computer typeset in Palatino 9 point by the Society of Saint Francis.
Cover emblem by Sister Regina OSB.

Printed by Martin's The Printers Ltd., Berwick upon Tweed

Preface

Prayer in the middle of the day has long been a part of the Christian tradition of daily prayer, and the desire to pause and worship God at a time when the busy-ness of life seems to be at its peak has been met by the enduring use of Psalm 119, perhaps the most meditative of the psalms.

The psalm was spread over the offices of Prime, Terce, Sext and None and recited in a day: its dwelling on God's ordinances and the desire to comply with them is its repeating theme, constantly drawing the one praying back to an understanding of God, of God's love for all he created and of creation's commitment to God. The psalms of ascent have been offered here as an alternative, and might be used at appropriate times and seasons.

One of the aims of the compilers of the full edition of *Celebrating Common Prayer* was to bring the daily prayer of the Church back to the people of God: not to take it away from clergy and religious, far from it, but to make it more easily accessible (in every sense of the word) to all worshipping Christians, whose rightful property it is.

It is with this in mind that this booklet has been produced; individuals or groups who wish to set aside a short time in the day, at a time suitable to them, will find here both psalms and readings to fix their prayer firmly in the tradition of daily prayer in the Church and also find hints in the readings and prayers which brings contemporary matters to mind. The danger with this latter provision is that such things quickly date, but if you find it so, don't let that be a hindrance or mar the process of prayer: the readings themselves are timeless meditations and stand in their own right; the essence is the offering to God in prayer.

CONTENTS

Sunday

THE PREPARATION

O God, make speed to save us.
O Lord, make haste to help us.

Glory to the Father, and to the Son,
  and to the Holy Spirit:*
as it was in the beginning, is now,
  and shall be for ever. Amen.

Alleluia! *(Omitted in Lent)*

A HYMN may be sung, the following or some other.

To God our Father, thanks and praise
For this, the first and dawn of days:
The day when through your word of might
From chaos was created light.

The day on which your well-loved Son
O'er death and hell the triumph won;
The day on which the Spirit came,
Your gift to us, in wind and flame.

To you, our Father, through your Son,
And in the Spirit, Three in One:
We, new-created on this day,
New songs of love and glory pay. Amen.

THE WORD OF GOD

Either: PSALM 119. 1-32

1   Happy are they whose way is blameless,*
    who walk in the law of the Lord!

2   Happy are they who observe his decrees*
    and seek him with all their hearts!

3   Who never do any wrong,*
    but always walk in his ways.

4   You laid down your commandments,*
    that we should fully keep them.

5   O that my ways were made so direct*
    that I might keep your statutes!

6   Then I should not be put to shame,*
    when I regard all your commandments.

7   I will thank you with an unfeigned heart,*
    when I have learned your righteous judgements.

8   I will keep your statutes;*
    do not utterly forsake me.

                    *   *   *

9   How shall the young cleanse their way?*
    By keeping to your words.

10 With my whole heart I seek you;*
    let me not stray from your commandments.

11 I treasure your promise in my heart,*
    that I may not sin against you.

12 Blessèd are you, O Lord;*
    instruct me in your statutes.

13 With my lips will I recite*
    all the judgements of your mouth.

14 I have taken greater delight in the way of your decrees*
    than in all manner of riches.

15 I will meditate on your commandments*
    and give attention to your ways.

16 My delight is in your statutes;*
    I will not forget your word.

                    *   *   *

17 Deal bountifully with your servant,*
    that I may live and keep your word.

18 Open my eyes, that I may see*
    the wonders of your law.

19 I am a stranger here on earth;*
    do not hide your commandments from me.

20 My soul is consumed at all times*
    with longing for your judgements.

21 You have rebuked the insolent;*
    cursed are they who stray from your commandments!

22 Turn from me shame and rebuke,*
    for I have kept your decrees.

23 Even though rulers sit and plot against me,*
    I will meditate on your statutes.

24 For your decrees are my delight,*
and they are my counsellors.

        *   *   *

25 My soul cleaves to the dust;*
give me life according to your word.

26 I have confessed my ways and you answered me;*
instruct me in your statutes.

27 Make me understand the way of your commandments,*
that I may meditate on your marvellous works.

28 My soul melts away for sorrow;*
strengthen me according to your word.

29 Take from me the way of lying;*
let me find grace through your law.

30 I have chosen the way of faithfulness;*
I have set your judgements before me.

31 I hold fast to your decrees;*
O Lord, let me not be put to shame.

32 I will run the way of your commandments,*
for you have set my heart at liberty.

Or:

PSALM 121

1 I lift up my eyes to the hills;*
from where is my help to come?

2 My help comes from the Lord,*
the maker of heaven and earth.

3 He will not let your foot be moved*
and he who watches over you will not fall asleep.

4 Behold, he who keeps watch over Israel*
shall neither slumber nor sleep;

5 The Lord himself watches over you;*
the Lord is your shade at your right hand,

6 So that the sun shall not strike you by day,*
nor the moon by night.

7 The Lord shall preserve you from all evil;*
it is he who shall keep you safe.

8   The Lord shall watch over your going out and your coming in,*
    from this time forth for evermore.

PSALM 122

1   I was glad when they said to me,*
    'Let us go to the house of the Lord.'

2   Now our feet are standing*
    within your gates, O Jerusalem.

3   Jerusalem is built as a city*
    that is at unity with itself.

4   To which the tribes go up, the tribes of the Lord,*
    the assembly of Israel, to praise the name of the Lord.

5   For there are the thrones of judgement,*
    the thrones of the house of David.

6   Pray for the peace of Jerusalem:*
    'May they prosper who love you.

7   'Peace be within your walls*
    and quietness within your towers.

8   'For my family and companions' sake,*
    I pray for your prosperity.

9   'Because of the house of the Lord our God,*
    I will seek to do you good.'

Each psalm, or group of psalms, may end with:

**Glory to the Father, and to the Son,
    and to the Holy Spirit:***
**as it was in the beginning, is now,
    and shall be for ever.   Amen.**

THE READING (Creation and New Creation)

Week 1:   Proverbs 8. 30-31
    2:   Genesis 2. 4-7
    3:   Matthew 6. 25-33
    4:   Romans 8. 19-21
    5:   2 Corinthians 5. 17
    6:   Colossians 1. 15-17
    7:   Revelation 21. 1-3

Or, the short reading:
Wisdom says: I was beside him like a little child, and I was
daily his delight, playing in his presence continually, rejoicing
in the inhabited world and delighting in the human race.

                                                Proverbs 8. 30-31

THE RESPONSE Either:

The wolf shall live with the lamb,
The leopard lie down with the kid;

The calf and the lion together,
And a little child shall lead them.

They will not hurt or destroy
On all my holy mountain.

For the earth will be full of the knowledge of God
As the waters cover the sea.

Or:

Blessèd are you, O God: Father, Son and Holy Spirit;
We give you praise and honour for ever.

For you have loved us from all eternity,
And remembered us when we were in trouble.

Blessèd are you, Lord Jesus Christ,
Who, for our salvation, came down from heaven.

By the power of the Holy Spirit,
You became incarnate of the Virgin Mary.

You loosed us from our sins by your own blood:
And on the third day rose from the dead.

You ascended up on high,
And opened wide for us the everlasting doors.

You are seated at the right hand of the Father
And ever live to intercede for us.

Blessèd are you, O God: Source of all being,
   eternal Word and Spirit of life;
We give you praise and honour for ever.

THE PRAYERS

Intercession and thanksgiving are offered in free prayer or in silence, ending with the following:

Lord, have mercy.
Lord, have mercy.

Christ, have mercy.
Christ, have mercy.

Lord, have mercy.
Lord, have mercy.

THE COLLECT: one of the following or some other.

Maker of all,
you have created the heavens and the earth
and made us in your own image:
may we discern your hand in all your works
and serve you with reverence and thanksgiving;
through Jesus Christ our Lord,
who with you and the Holy Spirit
reigns supreme over all things
now and for ever. **Amen.**   4

Or:

Almighty and eternal God,
strengthen our faith, we pray,
so that in this world
we may firmly believe and truly proclaim
   the Holy Trinity
and in the world to come know you perfectly
and with joy behold you face to face;
for you live and reign, one God,
now and for ever. **Amen.**   4

THE LORD'S PRAYER may be said.

[Rejoicing in God's new creation,
let us pray as our Redeemer has taught us:]

Our Father in heaven,	**Our Father, who art in heaven,**
hallowed be your name,	**hallowed be thy name;**
your kingdom come,	**thy kingdom come;**
your will be done,	**thy will be done;**
on earth as in heaven.	**on earth as it is in heaven.**
Give us today our daily bread.	**Give us this day our daily bread.**
Forgive us our sins	**and forgive us our trespasses,**
as we forgive those	**as we forgive those**
** who sin against us.**	** who trespass against us.**
Lead us not into temptation	**And lead us not into temptation;**
but deliver us from evil.	**but deliver us from evil.**
[For the kingdom, the power,	**[For thine is the kingdom,**
** and the glory are yours**	**the power, and the glory,**
now and for ever.] Amen.	**for ever and ever.] Amen.**

THE BLESSING

May God who made both heaven and earth bless us. **Amen.**

Let us bless the Lord.
Thanks be to God.

Monday

THE PREPARATION

O God, make speed to save us.
O Lord, make haste to help us.

Glory to the Father, and to the Son,
   and to the Holy Spirit:*
as it was in the beginning, is now,
   and shall be for ever. Amen.

Alleluia! *(Omitted in Lent)*

A HYMN may be sung, the following or some other.

Come, Holy Spirit, ever One
With God the Father and the Son:
Come swiftly, Fount of grace, and pour
Into our hearts your boundless store.

With all our strength, with heart and tongue,
By word and deed your praise be sung:
And love light up our mortal frame
Till others catch the living flame.

O Father, that we ask be done
Through Jesus Christ, your only Son,
Who, with the Spirit, reigns above;
Three Persons in one God of love. Amen.

THE WORD OF GOD

Either: PSALM 119. 33-56

33 Teach me, O Lord, the way of your statutes,*
   and I shall keep it to the end.

34 Give me understanding and I shall keep your law;*
   I shall keep it with all my heart.

35 Make me go in the path of your commandments,*
   for that is my desire.

36 Incline my heart to your decrees*
   and not to unjust gain.

37 Turn my eyes from watching what is worthless;*
   give me life in your ways.

38 Fulfil your promise to your servant,*
   which you make to those who fear you.

39 Turn away the reproach which I dread,*
   because your judgements are good.

40 Behold, I long for your commandments;*
   in your righteousness preserve my life.

*   *   *

41 Let your loving-kindness come to me, O Lord,*
   and your salvation, according to your promise.

42 Then shall I have a word for those who taunt me,*
   because I trust in your words.

43 Do not take the word of truth out of my mouth,*
   for my hope is in your judgements.

44 I shall continue to keep your law;*
   I shall keep it for ever and ever.

45 I will walk at liberty,*
   because I study your commandments.

46 I will tell of your decrees before kings*
   and will not be ashamed.

47 I delight in your commandments,*
   which I have always loved.

48 I will lift up my hands to your commandments,*
   and I will meditate on your statutes.

*   *   *

49 Remember your word to your servant,*
   because you have given me hope.

50 This is my comfort in my trouble,*
   that your promise gives me life.

51 The proud have derided me cruelly,*
   but I have not turned from your law.

52 When I remember your judgements of old,*
   O Lord, I take great comfort.

53 I am filled with a burning rage,*
   because of the wicked who forsake your law.

54 Your statutes have been like songs to me*
   wherever I have lived as a stranger.

55 I remember your name in the night, O Lord,*
and dwell upon your law.

56 This is how it has been with me,*
because I have kept your commandments.

Or:

PSALM 123

1 To you I lift up my eyes,*
to you enthroned in the heavens.

2 As the eyes of servants look to the hand of their masters,*
and the eyes of a maid to the hand of her mistress,

3 So our eyes look to the Lord our God,*
until he show us his mercy.

4 Have mercy upon us, O Lord, have mercy,*
for we have had more than enough of contempt,

5 Too much of the scorn of the indolent rich,*
and of the derision of the proud.

PSALM 124

1 If the Lord had not been on our side,*
let Israel now say;

2 If the Lord had not been on our side,*
when enemies rose up against us;

3 Then would they have swallowed us up alive*
in their fierce anger towards us;

4 Then would the waters have overwhelmed us*
and the torrent gone over us;

5 Then would the raging waters*
have gone right over us.

6 Blessèd be the Lord!*
he has not given us over to be a prey for their teeth.

7 We have escaped like a bird from the snare of the fowler;*
the snare is broken and we have escaped.

8 Our help is in the name of the Lord,*
the maker of heaven and earth.

Each psalm, or group of psalms, may end with:

**Glory to the Father, and to the Son,
and to the Holy Spirit:***
**as it was in the beginning, is now,
and shall be for ever. Amen.**

THE READING (Communication and Cultures)

Week 1: Habbakuk 2. 14
　　 2: Romans 2. 14-16
　　 3: John 4. 19-24
　　 4: Isaiah 52. 7-8
　　 5: Wisdom 7. 22-25
　　 6: Acts 2. 1-4
　　 7: Matthew 28. 18-20

Or, the short reading:
The earth shall be filled with the knowledge of the glory of God,
as the waters cover the sea.　　　　　　　　　 *Habakkuk 2. 14*

THE RESPONSE Either:

This is the sign of the Covenant
That I make between myself and you.

I set my bow in the clouds
The sign of the Covenant between us.

The Covenant between God and creation
And all that lives on the earth.

Or:

You are not in the flesh but in the Spirit
Since the Spirit of God dwells in you.

If Christ lives in you, though the body is dead because of sin,
The Spirit is alive because of righteousness.

If the Spirit of God who raised up Jesus from the dead lives in you,
God will give life to your mortal bodies also,
　　through the Spirit which lives in you.

For you are not in the flesh,
But in the Spirit.

THE PRAYERS

Intercession and thanksgiving are offered in free prayer or in silence, ending with the following:

Lord, have mercy.
Lord, have mercy.

Christ, have mercy.
Christ, have mercy.

Lord, have mercy.
Lord, have mercy.

THE COLLECT: one of the following or some other.

God of revelation,
whose mercy embraces all peoples and nations:
tear down the walls which divide us,
break open the prisons which hold us captive
and so free us to celebrate your beauty
in all the earth;
through Jesus, our Brother and our Redeemer. **Amen.** *1*

Or:

God in heaven,
may your Holy Spirit,
the Comforter who proceeds from you,
enlighten our minds,
lead us into all truth
and make us active in your service;
through Jesus Christ our Lord. **Amen.** *4*

THE LORD'S PRAYER may be said (see page 7).

[Being made one by the power of the Spirit,
let us pray as our Saviour has taught us:]

Our Father in heaven, *Or* **Our Father, who art in heaven,**

THE BLESSING

May God kindle in us the fire of love. **Amen.**

Let us bless the Lord.
Thanks be to God.

Tuesday

THE PREPARATION

O God, make speed to save us.
O Lord, make haste to help us.

Glory to the Father, and to the Son,
    and to the Holy Spirit:*
as it was in the beginning, is now,
    and shall be for ever. Amen.

Alleluia! *(Omitted in Lent)*

A HYMN may be sung, the following or some other.

O God of truth, O Lord of might,
You order time and change aright,
And send the early morning ray
And light the glow of perfect day.

Extinguish every sinful fire
And banish all our ill desire;
And, while you keep the body whole,
Shed forth your peace upon the soul.

O Father, that we ask be done
Through Jesus Christ, your only Son,
Who, with the Spirit, reigns above,
Three Persons in one God of love. Amen.

THE WORD OF GOD

Either: PSALM 119. 57-80

57 You only are my portion, O Lord;*
    I have promised to keep your words.

58 I entreat you with all my heart,*
    be merciful to me according to your promise.

59 I have considered my ways*
    and turned my feet towards your decrees.

60 I hasten and do not tarry*
    to keep your commandments.

61 Though the cords of the wicked entangle me,*
    I do not forget your law.

62 At midnight I will rise to give you thanks,*
    because of your righteous judgements.

63 I am a companion of all who fear you*
and of those who keep your commandments.

64 The earth, O Lord, is full of your love;*
instruct me in your statutes.

*   *   *

65 O Lord, you have dealt graciously with your servant,*
according to your word.

66 Teach me discernment and knowledge,*
for I have believed in your commandments.

67 Before I was afflicted I went astray,*
but now I keep your word.

68 You are good and you bring forth good;*
instruct me in your statutes.

69 The proud have smeared me with lies,*
but I will keep your commandments with my whole heart.

70 Their heart is gross and fat,*
but my delight is in your law.

71 It is good for me that I have been afflicted,*
that I might learn your statutes.

72 The law of your mouth is dearer to me*
than thousands in gold and silver.

*   *   *

73 Your hands have made me and fashioned me;*
give me understanding,
that I may learn your commandments.

74 Those who fear you will be glad when they see me,*
because I trust in your word.

75 I know, O Lord, that your judgements are right*
and that in faithfulness you have afflicted me.

76 Let your loving-kindness be my comfort*
as you have promised to your servant.

77 Let your compassion come to me, that I may live,*
for your law is my delight.

78 Let the arrogant be put to shame,
for they wrong me with lies;*
but I will meditate on your commandments.

79 Let those who fear you turn to me,*
    and also those who know your decrees.

80 Let my heart be sound in your statutes,*
    that I may not be put to shame.

Or:

PSALM 125

1 Those who trust in the Lord are like Mount Zion,*
    which cannot be moved, but stands fast for ever.

2 The hills stand about Jerusalem;*
    so does the Lord stand round about his people,
    from this time forth for evermore.

3 The sceptre of the wicked shall not hold sway
        over the land allotted to the just,*
    so·that the just shall not put their hands to evil.

4 Show your goodness, O Lord, to those who are good*
    and to those who are true of heart.

5 As for those who turn aside to crooked ways,
        the Lord will lead them away with the evildoers;*
    but peace be upon Israel.

PSALM 126

1 When the Lord restored the fortunes of Zion,*
    then were we like those who dream.

2 Then was our mouth filled with laughter,*
    and our tongue with shouts of joy.

3 Then they said among the nations,*
    'The Lord has done great things for them.'

4 The Lord has done great things for us,*
    and we are glad indeed.

5 Restore our fortunes, O Lord,*
    like the watercourses of the Negev.

6 Those who sowed with tears*
    will reap with songs of joy.

7 Those who go out weeping, carrying the seed,*
    will come again with joy, shouldering their sheaves.

The psalm, or group of psalms, may end with:

**Glory to the Father, and to the Son,
    and to the Holy Spirit:***
**as it was in the beginning, is now,
    and shall be for ever. Amen.**

THE READING (Wealth and Work)

Week 1: Colossians 3. 17
     2: Luke 13. 6-9
     3: Mark 10. 43-45
     4: James 5. 1-4
     5: 1 Timothy 6. 17-19
     6: 2 Corinthians 9. 6-8
     7: Matthew 11. 28-30

Or, the short reading:

Whatever you do, in word or deed, do everything in the name of the Lord Jesus Christ, giving thanks to God the Father through him.

Colossians 3. 17

THE RESPONSE *Either:*

Unless the Lord builds the house,
Those who build it labour in vain.

Unless the Lord defends the city,
The guard keeps watch in vain.

It is in vain that you rise up early
And go so late to rest.

Vain, also, to eat the bread of toil,
For God gives to his belovèd sleep.

The Lord shall preserve you from all evil;
Your Maker will guard your life.

God will keep your going out and your coming in,
Now and for evermore.

Or:

Behold, I send my messenger
  to prepare my way before me
And the One whom you seek
  will suddenly come to God's temple.

Who can endure the day of God's coming?
And who can stand when the Most High appears?

For God is like a refiner's fire and like fuller's soap
And shall sit as a refiner of silver
  and purify the offspring of Levi.

Who can endure the day of God's coming
  and who can stand when the Most High appears?
As for me, I will look to the Most High,
  I will wait for the God of my salvation.

THE PRAYERS

Intercession and thanksgiving are offered in free prayer or in silence, ending with the following:

Lord, have mercy.
Lord, have mercy.

Christ, have mercy.
Christ, have mercy.

Lord, have mercy.
Lord, have mercy.

THE COLLECT: one of the following or some other.

God of grace and goodness,
who made us body and spirit
that our work and faith may be one:
may we, by our life and worship,
join in your labour to bring forth a new creation
in justice, love and truth;
through Jesus, our Redeemer. **Amen.**   *1*

Or:

Stir up your power, O God,
and with great dominion come among us;
and, because we are sorely hindered by our sins,
let your bountiful grace and mercy
speedily help and deliver us;
through Jesus Christ our Lord. **Amen.**   *4*

THE LORD'S PRAYER may be said (see page 7).

[As we look for the coming of the Kingdom,
Lord, teach us to pray:]
Our Father in heaven, *Or* **Our Father, who art in heaven,**

THE BLESSING
May God bless the work of our hands. **Amen.**

Let us bless the Lord.
Thanks be to God.

Wednesday

THE PREPARATION

O God, make speed to save us.
O Lord, make haste to help us.

Glory to the Father, and to the Son,
   and to the Holy Spirit:*
as it was in the beginning, is now,
   and shall be for ever. Amen.

Alleluia! *(Omitted in Lent)*

A HYMN may be sung, the following or some other.

Lord Christ, you came on us to shine
True light from the eternal Light!
And now the Father's brightness rests
On those who long have dwelt in night.

O see how all that lives and breathes
True homage gives in deed and word:
The glory of almighty God,
The Father's image, Christ our Lord.

We bless the Father, Fount of light,
And you, O Christ, belovèd Son,
Who, with the Spirit, dwell in us;
The only God; the Three in One. Amen.

THE WORD OF GOD

Either: PSALM 119. 81-104

81 My soul has longed for your salvation;*
   I have put my hope in your word.

82 My eyes have failed from watching for your promise,*
   and I say, 'When will you comfort me?'

83 I have become like a leather flask in the smoke,*
   but I have not forgotten your statutes.

84 How much longer must I wait?*
   when will you give judgement
      against those who persecute me?

85 The proud have dug pits for me;*
   they do not keep your law.

86 All your commandments are true;*
 help me, for they persecute me with lies.

87 They had almost made an end of me on earth,*
 but I have not forsaken your commandments.

88 In your loving-kindness, revive me,*
 that I may keep the decrees of your mouth.

*   *   *

89 O Lord, your word is everlasting;*
 it stands firm in the heavens.

90 Your faithfulness remains from one generation to another;*
 you established the earth and it abides.

91 By your decree these continue to this day,*
 for all things are your servants.

92 If my delight had not been in your law,*
 I should have perished in my affliction.

93 I will never forget your commandments,*
 because by them you give me life.

94 I am yours; O that you would save me!*
 for I study your commandments.

95 Though the wicked lie in wait for me to destroy me,*
 I will apply my mind to your decrees.

96 I see that all things come to an end,*
 but your commandment has no bounds.

*   *   *

97 O how I love your law!*
 all the day long it is in my mind.

98 Your commandment has made me wiser than my enemies,*
 and it is always with me.

99 I have more understanding than all my teachers,*
 for your decrees are my study.

100 I am wiser than the elders,*
 because I observe your commandments.

101 I restrain my feet from every evil way,*
 that I may keep your word.

102 I do not shrink from your judgements,*
 because you yourself have taught me.

103 How sweet are your words to my taste!*
   they are sweeter than honey to my mouth.

104 Through your commandments I gain understanding;*
   therefore I hate every lying way.

Or:

PSALM 127

1 Unless the Lord builds the house,*
   their labour is in vain who build it.

2 Unless the Lord watches over the city,*
   in vain the guard keeps vigil.

3 It is in vain that you rise so early and go to bed so late;*
   vain, too, to eat the bread of toil,
      for he gives to his belovèd sleep.

4 Children are a heritage from the Lord,*
   and the fruit of the womb is a gift.

5 Like arrows in the hand of a warrior*
   are the children of one's youth.

6 Happy are they who have their quiver full of them!*
   they shall not be put to shame
      when they contend with their enemies in the gate.

PSALM 128

1 Happy are they all who fear the Lord,*
   and who follow in his ways!

2 You shall eat the fruit of your labour;*
   happiness and prosperity shall be yours.

3 Your wife shall be like a fruitful vine within your house,*
   your children like olive shoots round about your table.

4 Whoever fears the Lord*
   shall thus indeed be blessed.

5 The Lord bless you from Zion,*
   and may you see the prosperity of Jerusalem
      all the days of your life.

6 May you live to see your children's children;*
   may peace be upon Israel.

The psalm, or group of psalms, may end with:

**Glory to the Father, and to the Son,
   and to the Holy Spirit:***
**as it was in the beginning, is now,
   and shall be for ever. Amen.**

THE READING   *(Family and Community)*

Week 1:   Mark 3. 35
    2:   1 Samuel 18. 1-5
    3:   Genesis 1. 27-28
    4:   Matthew 19. 10-12
    5:   Mark 10. 13-16
    6:   Philippians 2. 1-2
    7:   Acts 2. 44-47

Or, the short reading:
Whoever does the will of God is my brother and sister and mother.
Mark 3. 35

THE RESPONSE   *Either:*

I bow my knees before the Father
From whom every family takes its name.

May we be strengthened in our inner being
With power through the Holy Spirit.

May Christ dwell in our hearts by faith
As we are being rooted and grounded in love.

May we know the love of Christ that surpasses knowledge
And be filled with all the fullness of God.

Or:

That which we heard from the beginning,
Which we saw with our own eyes and touched with our hands,

The Word of life, which was from the beginning,
We now proclaim to you.

The darkness is passing away
And the true light is already shining.

God is our light, in whom there is no darkness at all.
If we walk in the light, we have fellowship with Christ.

THE PRAYERS

Intercession and thanksgiving are offered in free prayer or in silence, ending with the following:

Lord, have mercy.
Lord, have mercy.

Christ, have mercy.
Christ, have mercy.

Lord, have mercy.
Lord, have mercy.

THE COLLECT: one of the following or some other.

Loving God,
from birth to death, you hold us in your hand:
make us strong to bear each others burdens
and humble to share our own,
that as one family
we may rest in your power
and trust in your love;
through Jesus Christ our Lord . . .   *1*

Or:

Almighty God,
you have shed upon us
the new light of your incarnate Word,
giving us gladness in our sorrow
and a presence in our isolation;
fill our lives with your light
until they overflow with gladness and with praise;
through Jesus Christ our Saviour. **Amen.**   *4*

THE LORD'S PRAYER may be said (see page 7).

[Rejoicing in the presence of God here among us,
let us pray in faith and trust:]

Our Father in heaven, *Or* **Our Father, who art in heaven,**

THE BLESSING

May Christ dwell in our hearts by faith. **Amen.**

Let us bless the Lord.
Thanks be to God.

Thursday

O God, make speed to save us.
O Lord, make haste to help us.

Glory to the Father, and to the Son,
  and to the Holy Spirit:*
as it was in the beginning, is now,
  and shall be for ever. Amen.

Alleluia! *(Omitted in Lent)*

A HYMN may be sung, the following or some other.

O God, creation's secret force,
Yourself unmoved, all motion's source,
Who from the morn till evening's ray
Through all its changes guide the day.

Grant us, when this short life is past
The glorious evening that shall last,
That, by a holy death attained,
Eternal glory may be gained.

O Father, that we ask be done
Through Jesus Christ, your only Son,
Who, with the Spirit, reigns above,
Three Persons in one God of love. Amen.

THE WORD OF GOD

Either: PSALM 119. 105-128

105 Your word is a lantern to my feet*
  and a light upon my path.

106 I have sworn and am determined*
  to keep your righteous judgements.

107 I am deeply troubled;*
  preserve my life, O Lord, according to your word.

108 Accept, O Lord, the willing tribute of my lips,*
  and teach me your judgements.

109 My life is always in my hand,*
  yet I do not forget your law.

110 The wicked have set a trap for me,*
   but I have not strayed from your commandments.

111 Your decrees are my inheritance for ever;*
   truly, they are the joy of my heart.

112 I have applied my heart to fulfil your statutes*
   for ever and to the end.

*   *   *

113 I hate those who have a divided heart,*
   but your law do I love.

114 You are my refuge and shield;*
   my hope is in your word.

115 Away from me, you wicked!*
   I will keep the commandments of my God.

116 Sustain me according to your promise, that I may live,*
   and let me not be disappointed in my hope.

117 Hold me up and I shall be safe,*
   and my delight shall be ever in your statutes.

118 You spurn all who stray from your statutes;*
   their deceitfulness is in vain.

119 In your sight all the wicked of the earth are but dross;*
   therefore I love your decrees.

120 My flesh trembles with dread of you;*
   I am afraid of your judgements.

*   *   *

121 I have done what is just and right;*
   do not deliver me to my oppressors.

122 Be surety for your servant's good;*
   let not the proud oppress me.

123 My eyes have failed from watching for your salvation*
   and for your righteous promise.

124 Deal with your servant according to your loving-kindness*
   and teach me your statutes.

125 I am your servant; grant me understanding,*
   that I may know your decrees.

126 It is time for you to act, O Lord,*
   for they have broken your law.

127 Truly, I love your commandments*
   more than gold and precious stones.

128 I hold all your commandments to be right for me;*
   all paths of falsehood I abhor.

Or:

PSALM 132

1   Lord, remember David,*
    and all the hardships he endured;

2   How he swore an oath to the Lord*
    and vowed a vow to the Mighty One of Jacob:

3   'I will not come under the roof of my house,*
    nor climb up into my bed;

4   'I will not allow my eyes to sleep,*
    nor let my eyelids slumber;

5   'Until I find a place for the Lord,*
    a dwelling for the Mighty One of Jacob.'

6   'The Ark! We heard it was in Ephratha;*
    we found it in the fields of Jearim.

7   'Let us go to God's dwelling place;*
    let us fall upon our knees before his footstool.'

8   Arise, O Lord, into your resting-place,*
    you and the ark of your strength.

9   Let your priests be clothed with righteousness;*
    let your faithful people sing with joy.

10 For your servant David's sake,*
    do not turn away the face of your anointed.

11 The Lord has sworn an oath to David;*
    in truth, he will not break it:

12 'A son, the fruit of your body*
    will I set upon your throne.

13 'If your children keep my covenant
       and my testimonies that I shall teach them,*
    their children will sit upon your throne for evermore.'

14 For the Lord has chosen Zion,*
    he has desired her for his habitation:

15 'This shall be my resting-place for ever;*
    here will I dwell, for I delight in her.

16 'I will surely bless her provisions,*
    and satisfy her poor with bread.

17 'I will clothe her priests with salvation,*
    and her faithful people will rejoice and sing.

18 'There will I make the horn of David flourish;*
    I have prepared a lamp for my anointed.

19 'As for his enemies, I will clothe them with shame;*
    but as for him, his crown will shine.'

**Glory to the Father, and to the Son,
    and to the Holy Spirit:***
**as it was in the beginning, is now,
    and shall be for ever. Amen.**

THE READING (Health and Healing)

Week 1: Matthew 15. 30
        2: John 5. 5-9
        3: Ecclesiasticus 38. 1-8
        4: Luke 7. 20-23
        5: 2 Corinthians 5. 1-5
        6: 2 Corinthians 4. 16-18
        7: Revelation 22. 1-2

Or, the short reading:
Great crowds came to Jesus, bringing with them the lame, the
maimed, the blind the mute and many others. They laid them at
his feet and he healed them.   *Matthew 15. 30*

THE RESPONSE Either:

Do not fear, for I have redeemed you,
I have called you by name; you are mine.

When you pass through the waters, I will be with you;
**And when you pass through rivers,
    they shall not overwhelm you.**

When you walk through fire, you shall not be burned:
And the flame shall not consume you.

Do not fear, for I am with you,
I am the Holy One, your Saviour. ·

Or:

Let us keep the unity of the Spirit in the bond of peace,
For there is one body and one Spirit,
  one hope of our calling.

There is one Lord, one faith, one baptism,
One God and Father of us all.

Grace was given to each of us
According to the measure of the gift of Christ.

He gave some to be apostles, some prophets,
  evangelists, pastors and teachers,
For building up the body of Christ.

Until we all attain to the unity of the faith,
To the knowledge of the Son of God.

No longer shall we be children, but fully mature,
Measured by the stature of the fullness of Christ.

THE PRAYERS

Intercession and thanksgiving are offered in free prayer or in silence, ending with the following:

Lord, have mercy.
Lord, have mercy.

Christ, have mercy.
Christ, have mercy.

Lord, have mercy.
Lord, have mercy.

THE COLLECT: one of the following or some other.

Heal us, O God, from all our afflictions
and keep us steadfast in your love;
bind up our wounds,
raise us from death
and lead us to fullness of life;
through Jesus Christ our Saviour. **Amen.**   *1*

Or:

God of glory,
you nourish us with your Word
which is the bread of life:
fill us with your Holy Spirit,
that through us the light of your glory
may shine in all the world;
for the sake of Jesus Christ our Lord . . .   *3*

THE LORD'S PRAYER may be said (see page 7).

[Let us pray for the unity of all peoples on earth,
in the words our Saviour has taught us:]

Our Father in heaven, *Or* **Our Father, who art in heaven,**

THE BLESSING

May Christ our redeemer make us whole. **Amen.**

Let us bless the Lord.
Thanks be to God.

Friday

THE PREPARATION

O God, make speed to save us.
O Lord, make haste to help us.

Glory to the Father, and to the Son,
  and to the Holy Spirit:*
as it was in the beginning, is now,
  and shall be for ever. Amen.

Alleluia! *(omitted in Lent)*

A HYMN may be sung, the following or some other.

We bless you, Father, Lord of life,
To whom all living beings tend,
The source of holiness and grace,
Our first beginning and our end.

We give you thanks, redeeming Christ,
Who bore the weight of sin and shame;
In dark defeat you conquered sin,
And death, by dying, overcame.

Come, Holy Spirit, searching fire,
Whose flame all evil burns away.
With light and love come down to us
In silence and in peace to stay.

We praise you, God, the Three in One,
Sublime in majesty and might:
You reign for ever, Lord of all,
In splendour and unending light. Amen.

THE WORD OF GOD

Either: PSALM 119. 129-152

129 Your decrees are wonderful;*
  therefore I obey them with all my heart.

130 When your word goes forth it gives light;*
  it gives understanding to the simple.

131 I open my mouth and pant;*
  I long for your commandments.

132 Turn to me in mercy,*
  as you always do to those who love your name.

133 Steady my footsteps in your word;*
   let no iniquity have dominion over me.

134 Rescue me from those who oppress me,*
   and I will keep your commandments.

135 Let your countenance shine upon your servant*
   and teach me your statutes.

136 My eyes shed streams of tears,*
   because people do not keep your law.

*   *   *

137 You are righteous, O Lord,*
   and upright are your judgements.

138 You have issued your decrees*
   with justice and in perfect faithfulness.

139 My indignation has consumed me,*
   because my enemies forget your words.

140 Your word has been tested to the uttermost,*
   and your servant holds it dear.

141 I am small and of little account,*
   yet I do not forget your commandments.

142 Your justice is an everlasting justice*
   and your law is the truth.

143 Trouble and distress have come upon me,*
   yet your commandments are my delight.

144 The righteousness of your decrees is everlasting;*
   grant me understanding, that I may live.

*   *   *

145 I call with my whole heart;*
   answer me, O Lord, that I may keep your statutes.

146 I call to you; O that you would save me!*
   I will keep your decrees.

147 Early in the morning I cry out to you,*
   for in your word is my trust.

148 My eyes are open in the night watches,*
   that I may meditate upon your promise.

149 Hear my voice, O Lord, according to your loving-kindness;*
   according to your judgements, give me life.

150 They draw near who in malice persecute me;*
   they are very far from your law.

151 You, O Lord, are near at hand,*
   and all your commandments are true.

152 Long have I known from your decrees*
   that you have established them for ever.

Or:

PSALM 129

1 'Greatly have they oppressed me since my youth',*
   let Israel now say;

2 'Greatly have they oppressed me since my youth,*
   but they have not prevailed against me.'

3 The ploughers ploughed upon my back*
   and made their furrows long.

4 The Lord, the Righteous One,*
   has cut the cords of the wicked.

5 Let them be put to shame and thrown back,*
   all those who are enemies of Zion.

6 Let them be like grass upon the housetops,*
   which withers before it can be plucked;

7 Which does not fill the hand of the reaper,*
   nor the bosom of him who binds the sheaves;

8 So that those who go by say not so much as,
   'The Lord prosper you.*
   We wish you well in the name of the Lord.'

PSALM 130

1 Out of the depths have I called to you, O Lord;
   Lord, hear my voice;*
   let your ears consider well the voice of my supplication.

2 If you, Lord, were to note what is done amiss,*
   O Lord, who could stand?

3 For there is forgiveness with you;*
   therefore you shall be feared.

4 I wait for the Lord; my soul waits for him;*
   in his word is my hope.

5 My soul waits for the Lord,
   more than the night-watch for the morning,*
   more than the night-watch for the morning.

6   O Israel, wait for the Lord,*
     for with the Lord there is mercy;

7   With him there is plenteous redemption,*
     and he shall redeem Israel from all their sins.

The psalm, or group of psalms, may end with:

     **Glory to the Father, and to the Son,
       and to the Holy Spirit:***
     **as it was in the beginning, is now,
       and shall be for ever.   Amen.**

THE READING (Caring for the Needy)

Week 1:   Galatians 6. 2
      2:   Deuteronomy 15. 7-8, 11
      3:   Deuteronomy 24. 21-22
      4:   Isaiah 58. 6-8
      5:   Luke 6. 32-36
      6:   2 Corinthians 8. 9, 13-15
      7:   Hebrews 13. 1-3

Or, the short reading:
Bear one another's burdens and so fulfil the law of Christ.

                                           Galatians 6. 2

THE RESPONSE   Either:

Come, you that are blessèd of my Father,
Inherit the kingdom prepared for you.

I was hungry and you gave me food,
I was thirsty and you gave me drink,

I was a stranger and you welcomed me,
I was naked and you clothed me,

I was sick and you took care of me,
I was in prison and you visited me.

As you did it to one of the least,
You did it to me.

Or:

The preaching of the cross is folly to those who are perishing,
But to those who are being saved, it is the power of God.

To those who are called,
Christ is the power of God and the wisdom of God.

For the folly of God is wiser than human wisdom,
And the weakness of God is stronger than human strength.

We adore you, O Christ, and we bless you;
Because by your holy cross, you have redeemed the world.

THE PRAYERS

Intercession and thanksgiving are offered in free prayer or in silence, ending with the following:

Lord, have mercy.
Lord, have mercy.

Christ, have mercy.
Christ, have mercy.

Lord, have mercy.
Lord, have mercy.

THE COLLECT: one of the following or some other.

Merciful God,
you loose the bonds of injustice
and let the oppressed go free:
give us the will to share our bread with the hungry
and to give shelter to the homeless poor,
for thus your glory shall be revealed;
through Jesus Christ our Lord . . .   *1*

Or:

May the power of your love, Lord Christ,
fiery and sweet,
so absorb our hearts
as to withdraw them from all that is under heaven;
grant that we may be ready
to die for love of your love,
as you died for love of our love. **Amen.**   *Francis of Assisi*

THE LORD'S PRAYER may be said (see page 7).

[Lord Jesus, remember us in your Kingdom
and teach us to pray:]

Our Father in heaven, *Or* **Our Father, who art in heaven,**

THE BLESSING

May Christ our Redeemer show us compassion and mercy. **Amen.**

Let us bless the Lord.
Thanks be to God.

Saturday

THE PREPARATION

O God, make speed to save us.
O Lord, make haste to help us.

Glory to the Father, and to the Son,
    and to the Holy Spirit:*
as it was in the beginning, is now,
    and shall be for ever. Amen.

Alleluia! *(omitted in Lent)*

A HYMN may be sung, the following or some other.

Christ yesterday and Christ today,
For all eternity the same,
The image of our hidden God:
Eternal Wisdom is his name.

Christ keeps his word from age to age,
Is with us to the end of days;
A cloud by day, a flame by night,
To go before us on our ways.

We bless the Father, Fount of light,
And you, O Christ, belovèd Son,
Who, with the Spirit, dwell in us;
The only God; the Three in One. Amen.

THE WORD OF GOD

Either: PSALM 119. 153-176

153 Behold my affliction and deliver me,*
    for I do not forget your law.

154 Plead my cause and redeem me;*
    according to your promise, give me life.

155 Deliverance is far from the wicked,*
    for they do not study your statutes.

156 Great is your compassion, O Lord;*
    preserve my life, according to your judgements.

157 There are many who persecute and oppress me,*
    yet I have not swerved from your decrees.

158 I look with loathing at the faithless,*
    for they have not kept your word.

159 See how I love your commandments!*
O Lord, in your mercy, preserve me.

160 The heart of your word is truth;*
all your righteous judgements endure for evermore.

*   *   *

161 Rulers have persecuted me without a cause,*
but my heart stands in awe of your word.

162 I am as glad because of your promise*
as one who finds great spoils.

163 As for lies, I hate and abhor them,*
but your law is my love.

164 Seven times a day do I praise you,*
because of your righteous judgements.

165 Great peace have they who love your law;*
for them there is no stumbling block.

166 I have hoped for your salvation, O Lord,*
and I have fulfilled your commandments.

167 I have kept your decrees*
and I have loved them deeply.

168 I have kept your commandments and decrees,*
for all my ways are before you.

*   *   *

169 Let my cry come before you, O Lord;*
give me understanding, according to your word.

170 Let my supplication come before you;*
deliver me, according to your promise.

171 My lips shall pour forth your praise,*
when you teach me your statutes.

172 My tongue shall sing of your promise,*
for all your commandments are righteous.

173 Let your hand be ready to help me,*
for I have chosen your commandments.

174 I long for your salvation, O Lord,*
and your law is my delight.

175 Let me live and I will praise you,*
and let your judgements help me.

176 I have gone astray like a sheep that is lost;*
    search for your servant,
        for I do not forget your commandments.

Or:

PSALM 131

1   O Lord, I am not proud;*
    I have no haughty looks.

2   I do not occupy myself with great matters,*
    or with things that are too hard for me.

3   But I still my soul and make it quiet,
        like a child upon its mother's breast;*
    my soul is quieted within me.

4   O Israel, wait upon the Lord,*
    from this time forth for evermore.

PSALM 133

1   O how good and pleasant it is,*
    when a family lives together in unity!

2   It is like fine oil upon the head*
    that runs down upon the beard,

3   Upon the beard of Aaron,*
    and runs down upon the collar of his robe.

4   It is like the dew of Hermon*
    that falls upon the hills of Zion.

5   For there the Lord has ordained the blessing:*
    life for evermore.

Each psalm, or group of psalms, may end with:

**Glory to the Father, and to the Son,
    and to the Holy Spirit:***
**as it was in the beginning, is now,
    and shall be for ever.   Amen.**

THE READING (Justice and Peace)

Week 1: Psalm 72. 7
    2: Isaiah 9. 6-7
    3: Isaiah 32. 16-18
    4: Isaiah 41. 17-18
    5: Isaiah 42. 1-4
    6: Isaiah 61. 1-3
    7: Micah 4. 3-4

Or, the short reading:
In those days shall the righteous flourish; there shall be
abundance of peace till the moon shall be no more.   *Psalm 72. 7*

THE RESPONSE Either:

Blessèd are you who are poor,
For yours is the kingdom of heaven.

Blessèd are you who hunger now,
For you will be fed.

Blessèd are you who weep now,
For you will laugh.

Blessèd are you when people hate you,
    and when they exclude you,
When they revile and defame you,

Rejoice in that day and leap for joy,
For surely your reward is great in heaven.

Or:

Awake, O sleeper, and arise from the dead,
And Christ shall give you light.

If you have been raised with Christ, seek the things that are above,
Where Christ is, who is seated at the right hand of God.

Set your minds on things that are above,
Not on things that are on the earth.

You have died,
And your life is hid with Christ in God.

When Christ who is our life shall appear,
Then you will appear with him in glory.

Awake, O sleeper, and arise from the dead,
And Christ shall give you light.

THE PRAYERS

*Intercession and thanksgiving are offered in free prayer or in
silence, ending with the following:*

Lord, have mercy.
Lord, have mercy.

Christ, have mercy.
Christ, have mercy.

Lord, have mercy.
Lord, have mercy.

THE COLLECT: one of the following or some other.

Lord, make us instruments of your peace:
where there is hatred, let us sow love;
where there is injury, pardon;
where there is doubt, faith;
where there is despair, hope;
where there is darkness, light;
where there is sadness, joy.
O Divine Master,
grant that we may not so much seek to be consoled
    as to console,
to be understood as to understand;
to be loved as to love.
For it is in giving that we receive,
it is in pardoning that we are pardoned
and it is in dying that we are born to eternal life. **Amen.**

Or:

Almighty and everlasting God,
you have stooped to raise fallen humanity
through your Son Jesus Christ,
born of the blessèd Virgin Mary:
grant that we who have seen your glory
    revealed in our human nature,
and your love made perfect in our weakness,
may daily be renewed in your image,
and conformed to the pattern of your Son,
    Jesus Christ our Saviour. **Amen.**   4

THE LORD'S PRAYER may be said (see page 7).

[As we await the fulfilment of the promise of glory,
let us pray for the coming of the Kingdom:]
Our Father in heaven, *Or* **Our Father, who art in heaven,**

THE BLESSING

May God lead us in the way of peace. **Amen.**

Let us bless the Lord.
Thanks be to God.